Handmade Tales 2

HANDMADE TALES 2

More Stories to Make and Take

Dianne de Las Casas

Illustrated by Stefan Jolet

AN IMPRINT OF ABC-CLIO, LLC
Santa Barbara, California • Denver, Colorado • Oxford, England

Library of Congress Cataloging-in-Publication Data

de Las Casas, Dianne.
   Handmade tales 2 : more stories to make and take / Dianne de Las Casas ; illustrated by Stefan Jolet.
      pages   cm
   Includes bibliographical references.
   ISBN 978-1-59884-973-8 (paperback) — ISBN 978-1-59884-974-5 (ebook)
  1. Storytelling.   2. Children's libraries—Activity programs.   I. Jolet, Stefan, illustrator.   II. Title.
   Z718.3.D433   2013
   027.62'51—dc23   2012047481

ISBN: 978-1-59884-973-8
EISBN: 978-1-59884-974-5

17 16 15 14 13   1 2 3 4 5

This book is also available on the World Wide Web as an eBook.
Visit www.abc-clio.com for details.

Libraries Unlimited
An Imprint of ABC-CLIO, LLC

ABC-CLIO, LLC
130 Cremona Drive, P.O. Box 1911
Santa Barbara, California 93116-1911

This book is printed on acid-free paper ∞
Manufactured in the United States of America

For Mary Jo Huff,
A wonderful storyteller, a caring mentor,
and a fabulous friend. I love you, girl!
—Dianne de Las Casas

For Abigail,
My awesome goddaughter.
You rock!
—Stefan Jolet

Contents

Acknowledgments   ix

Introduction   xi

3-2-1-0 . . . Rudolph!: A Draw and Tell Tale   1

3-2-1-0 . . . Santa!: A Draw and Tell Tale   3

Amy's Love: A Möbius Strip Tale   5

Baby J: A Fold and Roll Tale   9

BINGO: A Draw and Tell Tale   13

The Captain's Shirt, A Ghost Story: A Tear and Tell Tale   15

Cassidy's Bud: A Napkin Fold and Tell Tale   19

Edward's Pet: A Cut and Tell Tale   23

Fairy-Tale Flashcards: A Flashcard Story Game   27

The Frog Jumping Jamboree: A Fold and Jump Tale   31

George's Surprise: A Fold and Tell Tale   35

The Grumpy Leprechaun: A Cut and Tell Tale   37

Jack and the Beanstalk: A Paper Roll Tale   39

Little Riding Hood: A Paper Bag Tale   47

Maria's Dance: A Tear and Twist Tale   55

The Möbius Brothers' Circus: A Möbius Strip Tale   57

The Mouse's Wedding—Japan: A Paper Plate Cutting Tale   61

The Naughty (Knotty) Bunny: A Handkerchief Tale   65

Patty's Tale: A Paper Accordion Tale   69

Puppy and Bunny: A Towel Folding Tale   73

Shine So Bright: A String Tale   77

Story Spinner Game: A Fold and Spin Activity   81

Tina's Misadventure: A Paper Bag Tear and Tell Tale   85

The Tortoise and The Hare: A Paper Plate and Twine Tale   89

The Wide Mouth Frog: A Towel Folding Tale   93

Source Notes   97

About the Author and the Illustrator   101

Dianne de Las Casas's Libraries Unlimited Titles   103

Acknowledgments

The first edition of *Handmade Tales* was published in 2008. Since then, I have conducted *Handmade Tales* workshops throughout the United States and abroad. It's been so much fun sharing the tales with children, educators, librarians, and storytellers around the world. As with any book, there are so many people to thank. Contrary to popular belief, an author never writes a book alone. I have a team of people to acknowledge (in alphabetical order).

A special thank you to the following people:

ABC-Clio — My publisher. Thank you for believing in my books and for continuing to publish them!

Emma Bailey — Because you work behind the scenes in production, you don't always get the credit you deserve but I appreciate you so much!

Sharon Coatney (my amazing editor) — I have loved each and every book I do with you. You are not only my editor but now my dear friend!

Kendall Haven — If it weren't for you, I would not have had my first book published! I'm at #21 with this book, Kendall. Thanks and hugs!

Mary Jo Huff — This book is dedicated to you because you have dedicated your life to serving so many. You are a close friend and I love you!

Stefan Jolet — Thank you for always being there for me. You are an amazing graphic designer and illustrator. You RAWK.

Kat Mincz — For many years now, you have been an awesome librarian, cheerleader, and dear friend. Thank you for all you do!

David Titus — Your string figures always inspire me. Thank you for teaching me "The Star." You will always be a star in my book!

Teachers and Librarians — It is because of your countless requests for a second book that we are here with *Handmade Tales 2*. Thank you for encouraging me, inspiring me, and for giving me a reason to get "handy" again!

Finally, as always, thank you to my family: Antonio, Soleil, Eliana (my muse), Jennie, Pam, John, Jenevieve, Mom, Clay, Gary, and the James Kids: Christian, Jourdan, Camrynn, Ashlynn, and Jasmynn. I LOVE YOU!

Introduction

I have always been a storyteller. From the time I was a little girl, I loved reading and making up stories. I have always loved making things. I wouldn't call myself an artist, but I am certainly crafty. *Handmade Tales 2* is the best of both worlds.

I am always looking for new ways to tell stories. In *Kamishibai Story Theater*, I explored the Japanese art of picture telling. In *Tangram Tales*, I combined the ancient Chinese tangram with the ancient art of oral storytelling. In *A is for Alligator: Draw and Tell Tales from A–Z*, storytelling is combined with drawing to create unique tales that use every letter of the alphabet to create animals.

In my first *Handmade Tales* book, I explored cut and tell, draw and tell, string stories, fold and tell stories, and even stories made with dollar bills. The stories in *Handmade Tales* had to meet certain criteria. The materials used for the "handy" tales had to be readily available or inexpensive because they needed to work with large groups of children, educators, or librarians. It was the same with this second book. In addition to the cut and tell, draw and tell, and fold and tell tales, I added stories made with paper bags, paper plates, index cards, newspaper, and washcloths.

For those of you who adored "Bandana Man" from the first *Handmade Tales*, I think you will also love "Naughty (Knotty) Bunny," who is made with a bandana tied into knots. There are fun literacy games like "Fairy-Tale Flashcards" and "Story Spinners" that work well with groups of children. "The Möbius Brothers Circus" is so cool that it seems to have an element of magic when you tell the story. If you work with younger children, "George's Surprise" and "Edward's Pet" are adorable. Upper elementary children will want to master "Amy's Love," and "Baby J" is a crowd pleaser for everyone.

Many of these stories require little to no prep. You just need scissors, paper, and a marker. They are great "to-go" tales! Consider teaching *Handmade Tales* to middle grade and high school students in a workshop setting. Everyone can use the skill of keeping young children entertained! Think siblings or babysitting.

Please share your *Handmade Tales 2* successes with me! E-mail me at dianne@diannedelascasas.com or connect with me on Facebook: fanofdianne or Twitter: @AuthorDianneDLC

Happy Handmade Tales to you!

Warmly,

Dianne de Las Casas

www.diannedelascasas.com

3-2-1-0 . . . Rudolph!
A Draw and Tell Tale

Supplies Needed:
- Drawing surface
- Marker

Note from Dianne:
Draw and tell tales are so much fun! This Rudolph draw and tell tale will have the children setting out treats for their favorite reindeer. I don't reveal the character at the beginning. I save it for the kids to guess. They never get it wrong.

Story:
I'm going to draw a popular holiday character in just four easy steps using the numbers 0 through 3. First, we'll start with the number 0.

Next, I am going to use the number 1. I wonder what those ones will make?

From *Handmade Tales 2: More Stories to Make and Take* by Dianne de Las Casas. Santa Barbara, CA: Libraries Unlimited. Copyright © 2013.

Look at this. I am going to use the number 2. First, a backward number 2. Then a regular number 2.

Now it's time for the holiday fun! Check out the number 3. What do you see forming? Do you see that smile? Who is it? That's right . . . it's Rudolph!

[*Sing the song below to the tune of "The 12 Days of Christmas."*]

Under the Christmas tree, Santa left for Rudolph . . .

Three carrot sticks
Two juicy apples
One bowl of oats and . . .
Zero pieces of gum!

Do you know why Santa doesn't give Rudolph bubble gum? What happens if Rudolph is flying, and he blows a big bubble? It pops and covers his nose. Then what?! That's right. It would be disastrous. Let's just stick to carrots, apples, and oats for all the reindeer.

3-2-1-0 . . . Santa!
A Draw and Tell Tale

Supplies Needed:
- Drawing surface
- Marker

Note from Dianne:
I love draw and tell tales. This Santa draw and tell tale will have the kids counting down the days until Christmas! I don't reveal who I am drawing. I like to let the children guess. It's so much fun to do this draw and tell at the end of a holiday program.

Story:
I'm going to draw a popular holiday character in just four easy steps using the numbers 0 through 3. First, we'll start with the number 0.

Next, I am going to use the number 1. Can you guess what those ones will make?

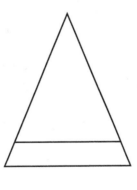

Now, I am going to use the number 2. Watch this! First, a backward number 2. Then a regular number 2.

Now it's time for the holiday magic! Check out the number 3! What do you see forming? That's right . . . a beard! And finally, a cotton ball on top of the hat. Who is this? You are so right. It's Santa Claus!

[*Sing the song below to the tune of "The 12 Days of Christmas."*]

Under the Christmas tree, Santa left for me . . .

Three hugs and kisses
Two snickerdoodles
One glass of milk and . . .
Zero crying kids!

Amy's Love
A Möbius Strip Tale

Supplies Needed:
- 1 sheet of red construction paper
- Stapler
- Tape
- Scissors

Note from Dianne:

This tale is best for upper elementary. Not only will they "get" the story line, they will be more likely to understand the concept of a Möbius strip. It is also a lot easier to teach upper elementary-aged children how to make this Möbius strip. It makes a great Valentine's Day story. Practice it a few times and you'll be rewarded with "oohs" and "aahs" from the kids!

Instructions:

1. Start with a sheet of construction paper in the landscape position.

2. Fold the sheet in half from top to bottom.

3. Fold the sheet in half again from top to bottom.

4. Cut the strips on the creases. There will be four. You need only two for the story.

You will begin the story with this step completed. The remaining instructions are within the story.

From *Handmade Tales 2: More Stories to Make and Take* by Dianne de Las Casas. Santa Barbara, CA: Libraries Unlimited. Copyright © 2013.

Story:
Amy was very lonely. More than anything, she wanted a companion.

[*Begin the story by holding up two strips, one for Amy and the other for the companion she wishes for.*]

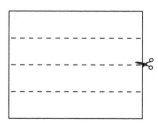

Amy was at a crossroads in her life. She needed to decide what to do.

[*Lay one strip on top of the other, creating a cross. Staple the cross at each corner.*]

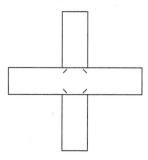

Amy was going crazy. She was so lonely. Her mind began to feel twisted.

[*Fold the right arm up.*]

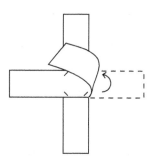

[*Turn the top corner down and attach it to the left arm with a piece of tape.*]

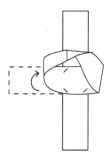

She began to think of how she would feel if only she had someone to spend time with, someone to go on long walks with. She wanted to find someone who loved her with all his heart. But Amy's heart was a tangled mess.

[*Flip the strips over.*]

[*Take the right arm and fold it down.*]

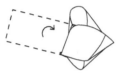

[*Turn the bottom corner up and attach the right arm to the left arm with a piece of tape.*]

So Amy decided to go for a walk in the park to clear her head. She followed the same path she had always taken. In fact, she walked for a very long time, thinking about her life. She walked until she came to the end of the path. That's when she saw HIM! Immediately she fell in LOVE!

[*Cut a little slit in the middle of the strip.*]

[*Continue cutting through the middle of all the strips.*]

She wasn't expecting it but there he was, perfect in every way.

[*When you are finished, you will have two intersecting Möbius hearts.*]

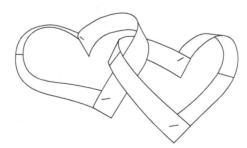

Amy took Harry to her house. That night she fed him. They snuggled on the sofa and watched old movies. Amy loved Harry, her new . . . DOG!

Baby J
A Fold and Roll Tale

Supplies Needed:
- 1 jacket
- 2 googly eyes
- Double-stick tape
- 1 pacifier with nipple cut off (optional)

Note from Dianne:
My niece Camrynn taught me how to make the jacket baby. It is very popular on playgrounds and would make a great prop for any story with a baby in it. I wrote this story especially for "The Jacket Baby." You will fold and roll as you tell. This one's for you, Cam!

Story:
Alexa was so excited. Her mom called and said she was bringing her and Nana a surprise! Alexa got dressed and put on her Sunday best.

[*Start with a jacket laid out flat with the arms open.*]

Alexa had a present for her mom, too! She began wrapping the present, folding the paper.

[*Fold the hood down.*]

She decided to add a ribbon to the present. She wrapped the ribbon around.

[*Fold right arm in, forming half of an X.*]

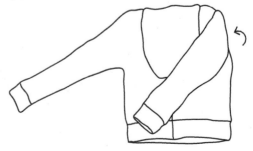

Then she added a bow!

[*Fold left arm in, forming an X.*]

Suddenly, Alexa heard a car roll into the driveway. Her mom was here!

[*Starting at the top of the jacket, roll down.*]

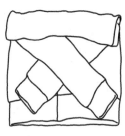

[*Continue rolling until jacket is completely rolled up.*]

Grandma and Alexa hurried to the door. There was her mom with the surprise in her arms.

[*Pull bottom of the jacket over all sides of the roll.*]

It was a baby brother!

[*Adjust the baby in the bundle and add googly eyes.*]

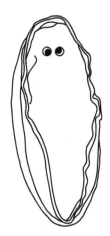

Alexa said, "Mom, I have a present for you too." Her mom unwrapped the present and discovered a pacifier for Baby J. Baby J opened his mouth and in went the pacifier! Alexa held her baby brother and smiled.

[*Hold the jacket baby and add a pacifier!*]

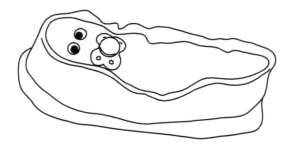

BINGO
A Draw and Tell Tale

Supplies Needed:
- Drawing surface
- Marker

Note from Dianne:
As a child, I always loved singing this classic tune. It's a school bus ride, campfire, classroom, and story time favorite. Now you can add a fun draw and tell element to the song. Sing it as usual, but draw as the kids sing. They will be amazed to see the letters turn into a dog!

Story:
There was a farmer who had a dog and BINGO was his name-o. B (*Draw the B*)-I-N-G-O, B-I-N-G-O, B-I-N-G-O, and BINGO was his name-o.

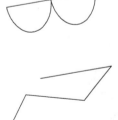

There was a farmer who had a dog and BINGO was his name-o. (*Clap*) I (*Draw the I*)-N-G-O, (*Clap*) I-N-G-O, (*Clap*) I-N-G-O, and BINGO was his name-o.

There was a farmer who had a dog and BINGO was his name-o. (*Clap*) (*Clap*) N (*Draw the N*)-G-O, (*Clap*) (*Clap*) N-G-O, (*Clap*) (*Clap*) N-G-O, and BINGO was his name-o.

There was a farmer who had a dog and BINGO was his name-o. *(Clap)* *(Clap)* *(Clap)* G *(Draw the G)*-O, *(Clap)* *(Clap)* *(Clap)* G-O, *(Clap)* *(Clap)* *(Clap)* G-O, and BINGO was his name-o.

There was a farmer who had a dog and BINGO was his name-o. *(Clap)* *(Clap)* *(Clap)* (Clap) O *(Draw the O)*, *(Clap)* *(Clap)* *(Clap)* *(Clap)* O, *(Clap)* *(Clap)* *(Clap)* *(Clap)* O, and BINGO was his name-o.

There was a farmer who had a dog and BINGO was his name-o. *(Clap)* *(Clap)* *(Clap)* *(Clap)* *(Clap)*, *(Clap)* *(Clap)* *(Clap)* *(Clap)* *(Clap)*, *(Clap)* *(Clap)* *(Clap)* *(Clap)* *(Clap)*, and BINGO was his name-o!

The Captain's Shirt, A Ghost Story
A Tear and Tell Tale

Supplies Needed:
- 1 large sheet of newspaper

Note from Dianne:
This story has been around in many versions. I heard a version of it when I was a little girl. All the versions I have heard were pretty simple. I have given the story a bit more suspense and a ghostly ending, which I think makes more sense of "The Captain's Shirt."

Story:
There was once a man who loved sailing the deep blue sea. His name was Captain Bayard. He was fearless and spirited.

[Start with a large sheet of newspaper.]

One day, he decided to search for treasure at the end of the world. He heard rumors of a big box filled with unimaginable riches.

[Fold newspaper in half from top to bottom with the crease at the top.]

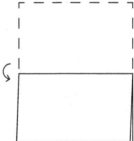

He had once sailed through and beyond the Bermuda Triangle, so nothing daunted Captain Bayard.

[Fold top right corner down to form a triangle leaving an inch edge at the bottom. Repeat with top left corner. Hold up paper for the audience to see the triangles.]

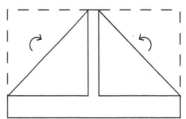

He packed his gear and made sure his boat was secure. When everything was in place, he was ready to set sail from Seaport, Maine.

[*Fold bottom edge up over triangles.*]

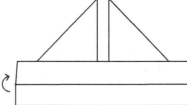

[*Turn paper over and repeat. Fold bottom edge up.*]

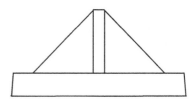

His boat, *The Seven Seas*, casted away on an uncharted adventure. He journeyed for days upon days. It was smooth sailing.

[*Hold the boat up and rock it across the waves.*]

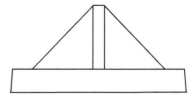

He was Captain Bayard, and nothing would stop him!

[*Hold the captain's hat over your head.*]

On the seventh day, his luck ran out. A storm brewed and gale winds made the sea angry. Brave Captain Bayard battled with all his might, but suddenly thunder roared and lightning cracked across the front of the boat, tearing off the bow.

[*Tear off left side of the boat.*]

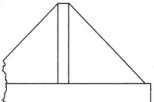

Captain Bayard held his breath as the tidal waves pounded the battered boat. The waves tossed the ship back and forth. A giant fist of water hammered the boat's stern, breaking it off completely.

[*Tear off right side of the boat.*]

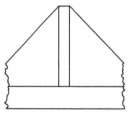

Captain Bayard was hanging on to his boat for dear life when another wave ripped away the boat's sails.

[*Tear off top of boat.*]

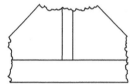

Captain Bayard yelled at the unrelenting sea. "I'm going down with my boat! Take meeeeeeeeee!" As if the ominous ocean was listening, another wave engulfed the captain, swallowing him whole.

When no one heard from the fearless captain, a search party was dispatched. All they found floating was . . . his shirt.

[*Open folds to reveal the captain's shirt.*]

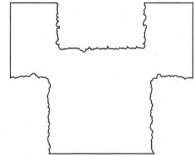

To this day, if you look into the ocean's horizon, you can see the silhouette of a mighty ship called *The Seven Seas*. And in the town of Seaport, Maine, people still talk in hushed tones and whispers about "The Captain's Shirt." Don't look behind you . . .

It just might float toward you, a grave reminder that the dead captain still searches for his lost ship.

[*Put on the shirt.*]

Cassidy's Bud
A Napkin Fold and Tell Tale

Supplies Needed:
- 1 fancy paper napkin with a repeating pattern

Note from Dianne:
This is a great story to teach kids to tell. If you are working with a larger group of children, you can also use plain, solid-color party napkins. The napkins should be stiff so that they can hold the folds. If you are doing this for story time, use a pretty patterned napkin.

Story:
Cassidy loved to garden. She had a little patch in her backyard that she tended.

[Fold a paper napkin in half diagonally, forming a triangle with the right angle pointing down.]

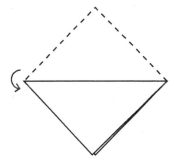

Every day, Cassidy came into the garden. She pulled the weeds. She watered the plants.

[Fold the top right corner down to the bottom point, forming a triangle. Repeat the step with the top left corner.]

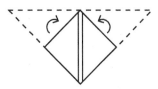

She was hoping to grow the prettiest flowers that she could enter into the botanical show. She wanted her flowers to win a prize!

[Fold the napkin in half from the bottom to the top.]

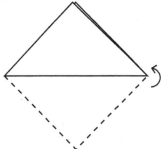

Cassidy went into her backyard every day to care for her little garden. But she did something special for her flowers. She talked to them and told them, "You are special little flowers. Grow for me. Grow!"

[*Fold the two upper layers down so that half the point protrudes below the bottom edge.*]

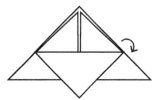

It seemed as though the flowers listened to Cassidy. They began to grow.

[*Fold the bottom point underneath the napkin.*]

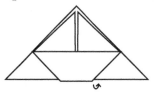

One day, Cassidy went into the garden and saw that buds were beginning to form. She was so excited. Soon, she would have beautiful blossoms to show off at the botanical show.

[*Turn the napkin over and tuck one of the side points into the other, forming a cylinder.*]

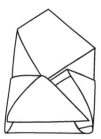

On the day of the botanical show, Cassidy went into her garden. Her pretty flowers were not yet ready. They were still baby buds!

[*Stand the napkin up with the cuffed edge in front.*]

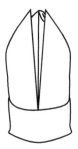

Cassidy said to them, "It doesn't matter that you are not fully grown. You are all still beautiful to me." She cut one of her prized flowers and placed it in a vase.

"You," she said to the bud, "are coming with me to the show." Cassidy proudly displayed her little bud at the botanical show.

[*Peel down the top two points to form petals on the bud.*]

Much to her surprise, Cassidy won a blue ribbon! Cassidy's bud won "Best Bud of the Show."

Edward's Pet
A Cut and Tell Tale

Supplies Needed:
- 1 8 ½ x 11" sheet of paper
- Marker
- Scissors

Note from Dianne:
This story is great for Pre-K through 2nd grade. Kindergarten through second graders can even make the elephant in the story. Special thanks to Pre-K teacher Nicole Pavich, from Lafayette Parish School System, for showing me the elephant. I added the story.

Story:
Edward wanted a pet so badly, but his mom would not let him have one. He begged and he pleaded, but still his mom said no. So Edward sat in his room and sulked.

[*Hold up sheet of paper in landscape position.*]

Edward said, "Mom, can I please have a dog? I'll take really good care of him!" But Edward's mom said . . . no.

[*Fold left side of sheet 1/3 of the way in.*]

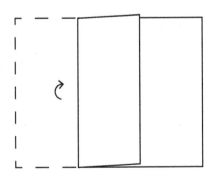

Edward said, "Mom, can I please have a cat? I'll take really good care of her!" But Edward's mom said . . . no.

[Fold right side of sheet 1/3 of the way in.]

Edward said, "Mom can I please have a fish? I'll take really good care of it!" But again Edward's mom said . . . no.

[Turn paper sideways and move it like a fish swimming.]

One day, Edward was in his room when he heard the doorbell ring. On his doorstep was a big box!

[Turn paper right side up again in the portrait position.]

It was for Edward! He couldn't wait to open it! He tore off the paper on one side of the box.

[Cut a small triangle off the top right-hand corner of the rectangle.]

Edward tore off the paper on the other side of the box.

[*Cut a small triangle off the top left-hand corner of the rectangle.*]

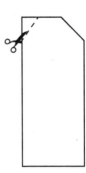

Edward lifted one side of the box.

[*About 1/3 of the way from the top of the rectangle, cut a long triangle off the bottom right-hand corner.*]

Edward lifted the other side of the box.

[*About 1/3 of the way from the top of the rectangle, cut a long triangle off the bottom left-hand corner.*]

Edward couldn't believe his eyes!

[*Open the flaps and in the middle, draw two eyes and the lines on the elephant's trunk.*]

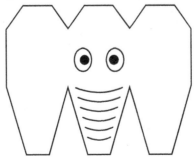

Edward had a new pet! It was an . . . [*show the audience the paper and let them chime in . . .*] ELEPHANT!
Edward hugged his mom and took good care of his . . . ELEPHANT!

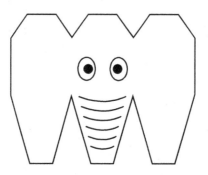

STOMP! STOMP!

Fairy-Tale Flashcards
A Flashcard Story Game

Supplies Needed:
- 2 sheets of 8 ½ x 11" cardstock
- Scissors
- 1 brad
- Black marker
- Hole punch

Note from Dianne:
So much of popular culture uses ancient folk and fairy tales as the foundation for parodies, books, and movies. This is a great way to familiarize children with popular fairy tales.

Flashcard Instructions:
1. Start with a piece of cardstock in the landscape position.

2. Fold the cardstock in half from side to side.

3. Fold the cardstock in half again from side to side.

4. Cut on the creases, creating four strips.

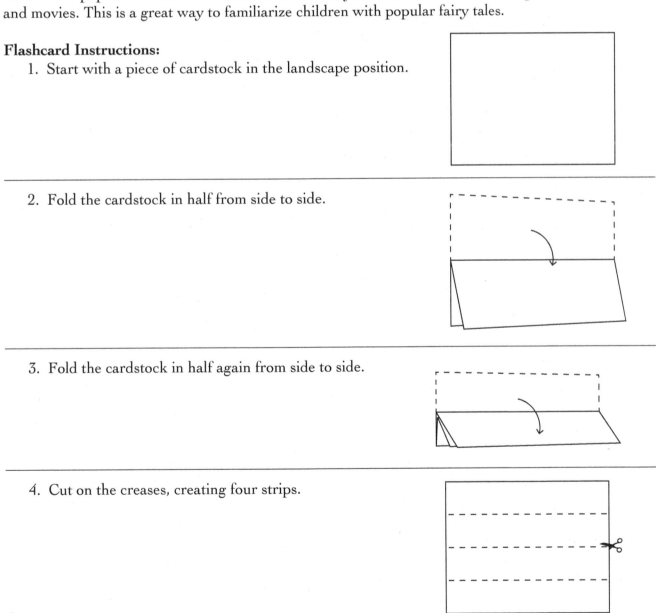

5. Hole punch the strips on the bottom.

6. Draw fairy-tale clues on each card. Use characters or major items from the fairy tales. Keep it simple, without too much detail.

7. Add a brad and secure the cards together.

Select List of Popular Folk and Fairy Tales:
- Aladdin
- Beauty and the Beast
- Cinderella
- Goldilocks and the Three Bears
- Hansel and Gretel
- Jack and the Beanstalk
- Little Mermaid
- Little Red Riding Hood
- The Frog Prince
- The Three Little Pigs
- The Little Red Hen
- Rapunzel
- Snow White

Game Instructions:
1. Have children sit in a circle.
2. Choose a child to be player one.
3. Fan out the cards with the clues facing you. The children will see the backside of the flashcards.
4. Have player one choose a card.
5. Turn it around and allow the child to guess the fairy tale. If they guess correctly, you can tell the story. Alternatively, have player one tell the story or have the children tell the story in a round-robin fashion, moving in a clockwise direction.
6. Once children have a mastery of popular fairy tales, play the game again, this time telling fractured fairy tales. You can read Jon Scieszka's *The Stinky Cheese Man* or Leah Wilcox's *Falling for Rapunzel* as examples.

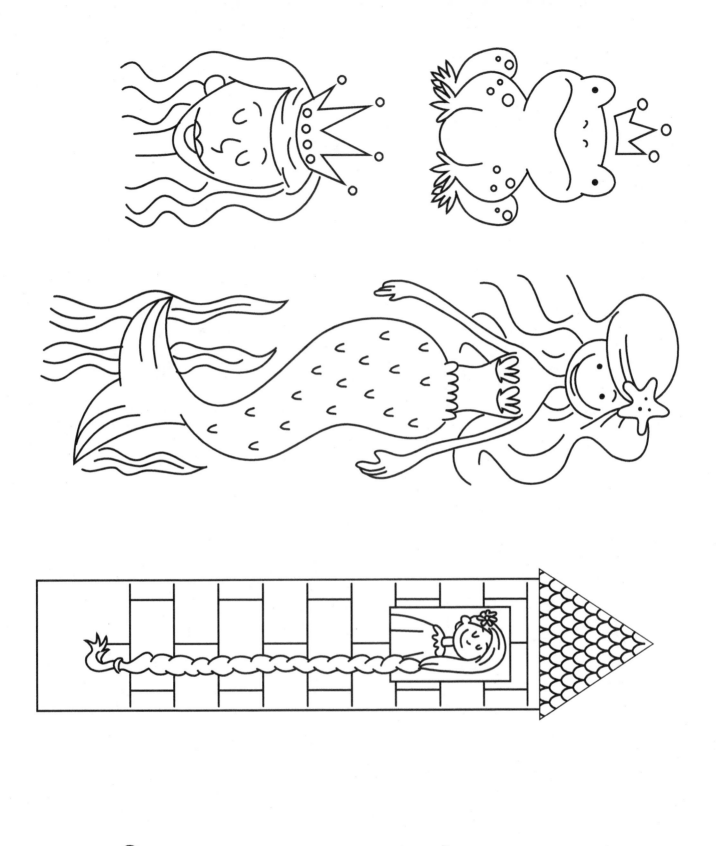

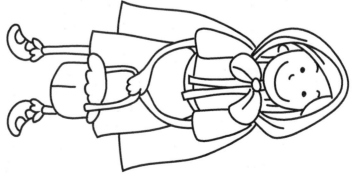

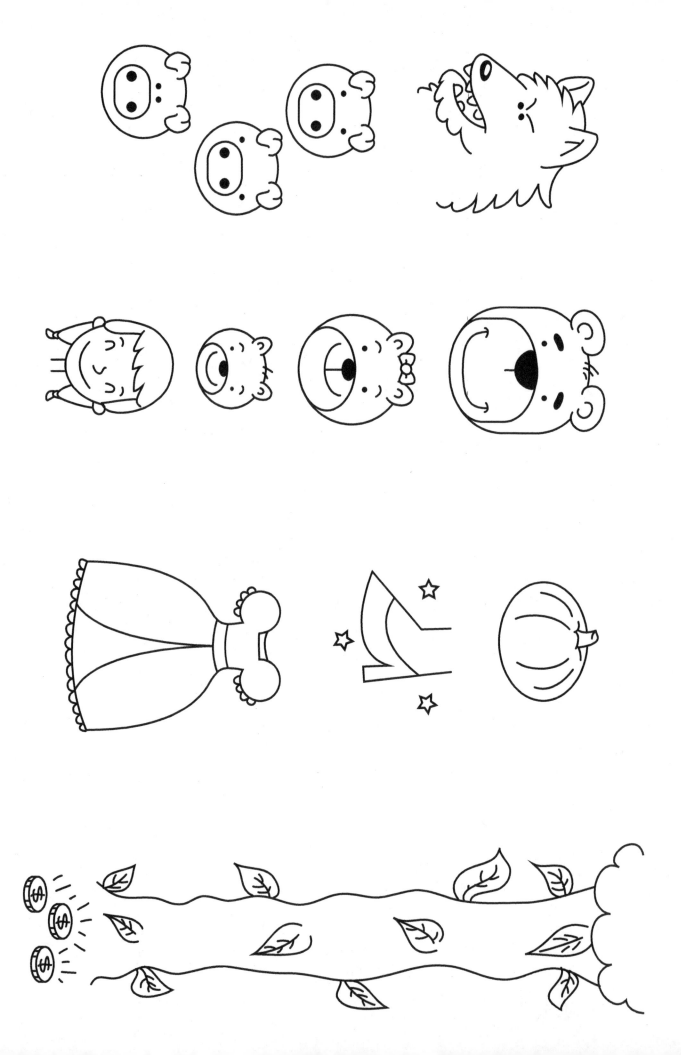

The Frog Jumping Jamboree
A Fold and Jump Tale

Supplies Needed:
- 2 colored 3 x 5" index cards
- "Medal" for the winner of the race
- Black marker (optional)

Note from Dianne:

I have been teaching children how to create this hopping origami frog for years. Rayne, Louisiana, is called the "Frog Capital of the World." They even have a frog jumping and racing contest. Every time I drive by Rayne, I say I want to write a frog jumping story. Well, here it is, combining my love of origami with a frog jumping jamboree. Make the frogs ahead of time. This is great fun to tell as the children race the frogs during the storytelling.

Frog Folding Instructions:

1. Start with a 3 x 5" index card in the landscape orientation.

2. Fold the card in half, lengthwise.

3. Fold down the top left corner to meet the bottom edge of the card, creating a triangle.

4. Fold up the bottom left corner of the card, creating a triangle.

5. Push in the sides of the creased X, forming a triangle at the top. It will look like a house with a roof.

6. Fold up each bottom corner of the top triangle, forming a diamond. This will become Froggy's feet.

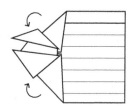

7. Fold the top and bottom edges inward to the middle.

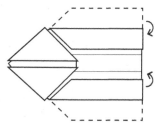

8. Fold the bottom edge to the tip of the triangle, folding the frog in half.

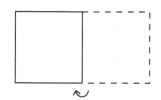

9. Fold back the top edge in half, creating the frog's back legs.

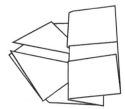

10. Decorate your frog. Make him hop by pushing down on his backside with one finger and letting go.

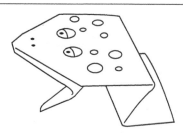

Story:
It was time for the annual Frog Jumping Jamboree. Nick and Justin couldn't wait to enter their frogs.

[*Have each child hold up their frog. You may want to make each frog in a different color so that you and the audience can differentiate between the frogs.*]

Though they were brothers, Nick and Justin had a competitive streak. Both of the boys really wanted to win. Not only would they gain bragging rights, they would win a year's worth of ice cream from the local soda shop!

[*Set the frogs on a table and create a start line and a finish line with colored tape. Gather children on both sides of the table to watch the race.*]

The announcer cried out and the buzzer sounded. It was time for the frogs to jump.

[*Sound an alarm like a bell. You are the announcer, so you have to narrate the race. You can change the characters' names to be the children you choose to participate in the story. The characters can also be girls. They don't have to remain boys.*]

The audience began cheering!

"Hop, frogs, hop
And don't you stop!
Hop, frogs, hop
And don't you stop!"

[*Encourage the children to chant as the race progresses. If a frog hops off the table, the race is over and the frog on the table wins. Explain this rule at the beginning of the race.*]

The boys raced their frogs, prodding them to hop.

The audience continued cheering!

"Hop, frogs, hop
And don't you stop!
Hop, frogs, hop
And don't you stop!"

The frogs continued jumping. Nick and Justin seemed to jump, too. The audience cheered on the frogs.

"Hop, frogs, hop
And don't you stop!
Hop, frogs, hop
And don't you stop!"

Finally, there was a clear winner. Nick's frog edged out Justin's frog in the race. Justin's face fell and he stared at the ground.

[*Have each child act out these parts.*]

When Nick was awarded the medal, he said, "I would like to dedicate this medal to my brother, Justin, the best brother in the world."

[*Hand "Nick" the medal. Have him put it around "Justin's" head.*]

Justin beamed, and Nick smiled. Clearly both brothers were winners.

[*Have boys high-five each other.*]

It was a great day at the Frog Jumping Jamboree because everyone lived . . . "hoppily" ever after. Ribbit. Ribbit.

George's Surprise
A Fold and Tell Tale

Supplies Needed:
- 1 sheet of construction paper
- Scissors
- Black marker
- Double-stick tape (optional, to tape down the ears and snout)

Note from Dianne:
This story is great to tell to Pre-K through 3rd grades. They will love the surprise ending! If you would like to teach the children how to make the dog, the folds are easy enough for children Kindergarten through 3rd grade to master.

Instructions:
1. Start with a sheet of construction paper in the landscape position.

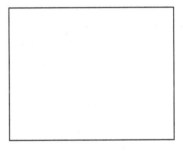

2. Fold the bottom left corner up, creating a triangle. Cut off the rectangular strip.

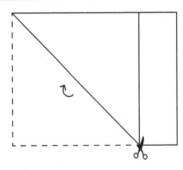

3. Turn the triangle so that the right angle points down.

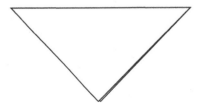

You will begin the story with this step completed. The remaining instructions are within the story.

Story:
Antonio lived in a big house. But he was lonely, because he didn't have any brothers or sisters.

[*Fold down the top right corner to create a triangle.*]

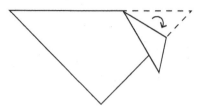

So Antonio decided to visit his best friend, George. He went to George's house and knocked on the door, but George was not there.

[*Fold the top left corner down to create a triangle.*]

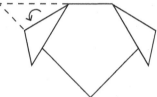

Antonio walked back to his house feeling very lonely.

[*Fold the bottom corner up, creating a triangle.*]

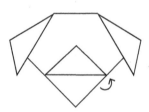

A few minutes later, the doorbell rang. George was on Antonio's front step with a basket!

[*Fold the top of the triangle down and tuck it inside.*]

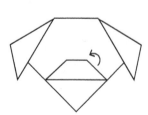

Inside the basket was a surprise!

[*Draw eyes, a nose, freckles, and a tongue.*]

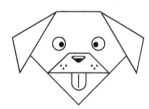

George brought Antonio a new friend. It was a wiggly, waggly . . . puppy!

[*Hold the puppy up for the audience to see.*]

The Grumpy Leprechaun
A Cut and Tell Tale

Supplies Needed:
- 1 large paper plate
- Scissors

Note from Dianne:
This is a fun St. Patrick's Day tale. I love the simplicity of the shamrock. If you are instructing younger children how to cut the shamrock, be sure they leave some paper plate attached at the bottom of the heart or they will end up with four separate hearts.

Story:
Katelin was walking through the meadow when she spied a little man with a big head sleeping.

[*Start with a large paper plate.*]

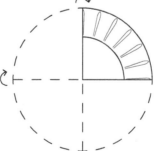

She asked, "What are you doing?"

The little man, who was a leprechaun, woke up startled and grumpy. He said, "What does it look like I'm doing?! I was taking a nap!"

[*Fold the paper plate into quarters.*]

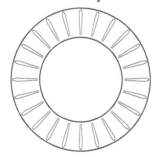

Katelin smiled. "Well, would you like to play? I'd love for you to be my friend."

[*Starting at the bottom, cut the shape of a heart, leaving a one-half inch of paper plate attached on each side of bottom of the heart.*]

When the leprechaun saw the girl's smile, he smiled back and felt a warmth inside his heart.

[*The finished heart shape.*]

The leprechaun answered, "I'd love to play with you but first, I have a surprise for you." He opened his hand and inside, was the prettiest little green flower with leaves in the shapes of hearts. "This shamrock will always bring you luck." Katelin tucked the unusual flower in her hair and grabbed the leprechaun's hand.

[*Open the heart to reveal a lucky shamrock.*]

They skipped through the meadow and danced underneath a rainbow.

Jack and the Beanstalk
A Paper Roll Tale

Supplies Needed:
- 11 feet of butcher block or continuous computer paper (5 ½ feet for the beanstalk, 5 ½ feet for the giant)
- Cardboard wrapping paper roll
- 1 8 ½ x 11" piece of cardstock for Jack
- 1 jumbo craft stick

- Bandana
- Tape
- Double-stick tape
- Marker
- Scissors

Note from Dianne:

This is a fun story time tale with the tall beanstalk, a GIANT giant, and fun audience participation! To create the giant's wife, fold the bandana in half, creating a triangle. Place the bandana on the head tying it under the chin to create a bonnet. I have condensed the original story a bit, otherwise, it would be an hour-long story!

Beanstalk Instructions:

1. Attach 5 ½ feet of butcher block paper to a cardboard wrapping paper roll

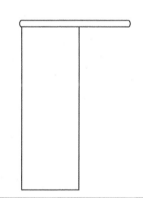

2. With a black marker, draw a beanstalk the entire length of the paper.

3. Cut five slits going up the beanstalk to insert Jack. Make sure there is one at the very top.

Giant Instructions:

1. With a black marker, draw a giant the entire length of the paper.

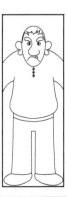

2. Attach to backside of beanstalk.

Jack Instructions:

1. Using half of an 8 ½ x 11" piece of cardstock, draw a 7–8" Jack.

2. Cut Jack out and attach a craft stick to the back side of Jack.

3. Now you have Jack and the Giant!

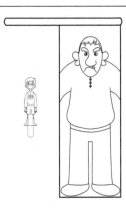

Storage Instructions:

1. Roll paper around the cardboard tube and secure with a rubber band.

2. Insert Jack into the rubber band.

Story:

This is a tale of wonder and magic, and I have no doubt that you will have fun journeying with me!

There was once a poor widow who had an only son named Jack. They had a cow named Milky-White. One morning, Milky-White gave no more milk. So Jack's mother decided to sell the cow. She sent Jack to the market with the cow. She said, "Don't do anything foolish, Jack. Sell Milky-White and we will be alright."

Jack nodded and led the cow down the road. It wasn't long before they met a man on the side of the road.

"Good day, young lad," he said to Jack. "Where are you headed?"

Jack answered, "I am going to the market to sell Milky-White."

The man said, "I will trade you your bonny cow for these magic beans. If you plant them overnight, by morning, a stalk shall grow right up to the sky, to the Land of the Great Beyond, where riches abound!"

Jack's excitement grew. "Yes, I'll do it!" he exclaimed. "I shall trade Milky-White for your magic beans." The deal was made, and Jack walked home with a small leather pouch full of beans.

When he arrived home, Jack said, "Mama, I traded our bonny cow for these magic beans!"

"Oh Jack! You are a fool. These are no magic beans. You have been swindled. Now we have nothing!" She tossed the beans out the window and said, "Not a sip shall you drink and not a bit shall you swallow tonight."

Jack went to his room and fell asleep with his tummy rumbling loudly. Overnight, a beanstalk began to grow and grow and grow and grow and grow!

[*As you are telling this part, slowly unroll the beanstalk until the whole beanstalk is revealed.*]

In the morning, Jack couldn't believe his eyes. He saw the . . . [*Pause so that the children can chime in.*] beanstalk!

Jack said, "I shall travel to the Land of the Great Beyond and bring mother back the riches she deserves." Jack began climbing the beanstalk, one foot above the other.

[*Place Jack in a slit at the bottom of the beanstalk.*]

Now, I'm going to need your help getting Jack up the beanstalk. Join in with me!

"Climb, Jack, climb!
Up, up, up!
Climb, Jack, climb!
Up, up, up!"

[*Repeat it a couple of times so that the children can catch on. Then move Jack up to a higher slit.*]

Jack got a little higher but we still need to help him. Let's go!

"Climb, Jack, climb!
Up, up, up!
Climb, Jack, climb!
Up, up, up!"

[*You can even have the children help you move Jack up the beanstalk.*]

Uh-oh. Jack still isn't at the top! Let's help him some more.

"Climb, Jack, climb!
Up, up, up!
Climb, Jack, climb!
Up, up, up!"

[*Move Jack to a higher slit.*]

Is Jack at the top yet? [*Allow children to chime in, "No!"*] Let's help him climb up!

"Climb, Jack, climb!
Up, up, up!
Climb, Jack, climb!
Up, up, up!"

[*Move Jack to a higher slit.*]

Jack is almost there! Don't give up! Let's help give him one last boost!

"Climb, Jack, climb!
Up, up, up!
Climb, Jack, climb!
Up, up, up!"

[Move Jack to the highest slit.]

Yay! Jack made it! When Jack reached the top, he followed a road that led him to a great big house. On the doorstep was a great big woman.

[Place the bandana on your head or the head of a child to play the giant's wife.]

"Good morning, mum," he said politely. "Would you be so kind as to give me some breakfast? My tummy rumbles loudly and I have not had a sip of drink nor a bit to swallow in quite some time."

The woman was the wife of an enormous giant. She had a soft spot for little boys. "Alright. I will feed you, but hurry because my husband does not like boys. If you hear him, hide in the oven."

No sooner had Jack finished his meal when he heard,

"THUD. THUD. THUD.
THUD. THUD. THUD."

Jack jumped into the oven and hid. The giant sat at the table. Jack's eyes grew wide as the giant began sniffing the air.

"Fee Fi Fo Foy.
I smell the blood of an English boy
Be he alive or be he dead,
I'll grind his bones to make my bread."

[Say to the children, "Let's say it together" and repeat the refrain, allowing them to join in. Allowing the children to participate makes it less scary, especially for the younger ones.]

The giant's wife said, "I am sure you are just imagining things. Why don't you take a nap?"

The giant grunted and left the table. Jack was just about to run away when the great big woman said, "Wait until he is asleep to sneak out."

So Jack waited. The giant went to a big chest and brought out three bags of gold, a golden egg-laying hen, and a singing harp. Holding his riches, he began snoring.

Jack crept out of the oven and carefully pried a bag of gold, the golden egg-laying hen, and the singing harp from the giant's arm. Jack stuffed them in a bag and ran as fast as he could with the bag over his shoulder.

But the harp cried out, "Master! Master!"

The giant awoke with a roar. "Stop you little thief. I shall grind your bones when I get a hold of you!"

Jack sprinted all the way to the beanstalk with the golden harp in tow. He began climbing down.

[*Place Jack in a slit at the top of the beanstalk.*]

Uh-oh! The giant is chasing Jack. He needs help getting down the beanstalk! Join in with me!

> "Climb, Jack, climb!
> Down, down, down!
> Climb, Jack, climb!
> Down, down, down!"

[*Move Jack down to a lower slit.*]

The giant is still coming. [*Flip the paper around so the children can see the giant. Then flip it back to the beanstalk.*] We have to hurry! Let's go!

> "Climb, Jack, climb!
> Down, down, down!
> Climb, Jack, climb!
> Down, down, down!"

The giant is fast behind Jack! [*Flip the paper around so the children can see the giant. Then flip it back to the beanstalk.*] Oh no! Jack still isn't at the bottom! Let's help him some more.

[*Move Jack down to a lower slit.*]

> "Climb, Jack, climb!
> Down, down, down!
> Climb, Jack, climb!
> Down, down, down!"

[*Move Jack to a lower slit.*]

Aaaah! The giant is still chasing Jack! [*Flip the paper around so the children can see the giant. Then flip it back to the beanstalk.*] Is Jack at the bottom yet? [*Allow children to chime in, "No!"*] Let's help him climb down and beat that giant!

> "Climb, Jack, climb!
> Down, down, down!
> Climb, Jack, climb!
> Down, down, down!"

[*Move Jack to a lower slit.*]

That giant just won't give up! Will he catch Jack? [*Flip the paper around so the children can see the giant. Then flip it back to the beanstalk.*] No! Jack is almost there! Are we going give up?! No! Let's cheer him on!

"Climb, Jack, climb!
Down, down, down!
Climb, Jack, climb!
Down, down, down!"

[*Move Jack to the bottom slit.*]

Yay! You helped Jack reach the bottom, but it isn't over yet! The giant did not give up easily. When Jack reached the bottom, he yelled, "Mama, Mama! Get me the axe!"

Jack handed the bag to his mother and took the axe from her. He furiously chopped down the thick stalk.

"Thunk, thunk, thunk, thunk, thunk!" The stalk began to sway. [*Wave the beanstalk from side to side.*]

The giant tried to climb back up, but it was all in vain. The beanstalk began to shiver and shake. Then it fell to the ground with a very loud THUD. [*Show the giant falling to the ground. Lay him flat.*]

Jack showed his mother the golden harp, which now called Jack "Master." With the gold, the golden egg-laying hen, and the singing harp, Jack gave his mother all the riches she deserved. Jack went to bed every night with a sip of drink, a bit to swallow, and a very full belly. And they lived . . . [*Allow children to chime in.*] happily ever after! The end!

Little Riding Hood
A Paper Bag Tale

Supplies Needed:
- 3 large paper bags
- 2 bandanas
- Scissors
- 2–4 rubber bands
- Black marker
- Stapler
- Tape

Note from Dianne:

I love how the costumes come out for this story. Little Riding Hood and the wolf are made out of paper bags. To create granny, fold a bandana in half to create a triangle. Place the bandana on the head and tie it under the chin, like a bonnet. For the woodsman, fold a bandana in half to create a triangle and tie it around the neck. Make the cape, the basket, and wolf as you tell the story. The kids will love seeing the paper bag transform. The wolf's nose is a little more time-consuming, so it can be made ahead of time. This is a great story to have the children act out with you. The paper bag costumes fit very well on children.

Hooded Cape Instructions:

1. Lay a paper bag flat, with the bottom of the paper bag at the top and facing away from you.

2. Cut a slit up the middle of the paper bag to the natural horizontal crease in the bag.

3. Continue cutting an oval shape (for the face), leaving about an inch of paper bag around the perimeter.

4. Cut slits on the side of the middle of the paper bag for the arms. Cut all the way up to the first natural horizontal crease in the paper bag. Do this on both sides of the paper bag.

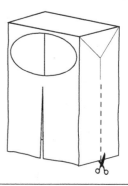

5. Place the "hooded cape" on a child. Secure the front of the cape with a piece of tape. This is the basic shape for any paper bag costume and can be repurposed to suit your needs.

Basket Instructions:
1. Lay a paper bag flat, with the bottom of the paper bag at the top and facing away from you.

2. Cut the paper bag in half.

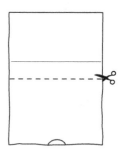

3. Open the bag and roll one cuff down around the edge of the bag.

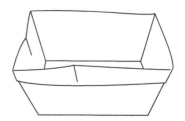

4. Using the excess paper bag, cut a 1 ½" wide strip. Do not cut the strip apart. Keep the loop. This will become the basket's handle.

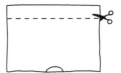

5. Place the paper strip loop around the middle of the bag making sure the bag is inserted lengthwise. Staple the strip to the cuff of the bag, creating the basket's handle. If you are going to place objects inside the bag, you may want to reinforce the handle with another strip loop and staple securely.

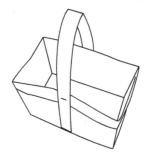

6. Pair hooded cape costume and bag and you have Little Riding Hood!

Wolf Instructions:

1. Lay a paper bag flat, with the bottom of the paper bag at the top and facing away from you.

2. Cut a slit up the middle of the paper bag to the natural horizontal crease in the bag.

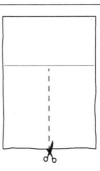

3. Continue cutting an oval shape (for the face), leaving about an inch of paper bag around the perimeter.

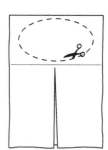

4. Cut slits on the side of the middle of the paper bag for the arms. Cut all the way up to the first natural horizontal crease in the paper bag. Do this on both sides of the paper bag.

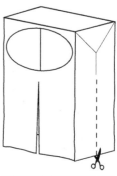

5. At the top of the paper bag (formerly the bottom), cut two tall triangles for the wolf's ears. Leave the bottom of the triangle attached to the bag.

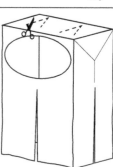

6. Stand both ears up. Place the "wolf" costume on a child. Secure the front with a piece of tape.

Wolf's Nose Instructions:
1. Using the oval you cut out from the face, cut an arch shape to create the wolf's snout.

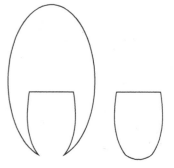

2. Draw a black nose at the end of the snout.

---

3. Create slits on each side of the top of the nose. Thread two to four rubber bands on each side, depending on the child's head size.

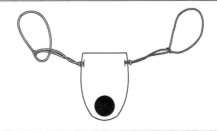

---

4. Loop the rubber bands around the child's ears. There should be slack in the rubber bands.

---

5. Pair wolf head and body costume with the nose. Now howl!

Story:
Deep, deep, way deep in the woods, there lived a pretty little girl who was loved by everyone, especially her Granny.

The little girl's mother called her over and gave her a beautiful cape with a hood. The girl was so fond of it that she wore it all the time. So she became known as Little Riding Hood.

One day, her mother called, "Little Riding Hood!"

Little Riding Hood listened to her mother and came at once. "Yes, Mama, what is it?"

Mama handed Little Riding Hood a big basket from which delicious aromas floated through the air. The basket was filled with freshly baked bread and homemade jam. Her mother said, "This is for Granny. I need you to deliver this gift."

Little Riding Hood said,
"Freshly baked bread and homemade jam

I'm Little Riding Hood, yes I am!"

Mama said, "Yes, but listen, my child. Hurry and bring it to her, quick, quick, quick. Be careful and don't stop along the way."

"Yes, Mama," said Little Riding Hood, and she set out for her grandmother's house.

Granny lived deep, deep, way deep in the woods, far from Little Riding Hood's house. It was a long walk. By and by, she came upon a big wolf. She did not know what a malicious beast he was so she was not at all afraid. "Hello, Wolf."

"How are you, Little Riding Hood?" the big wolf responded. "Where are you headed to with that big basket?"

"Oh, I am going to my Granny's house to deliver a gift."

"Freshly baked bread and homemade jam
I'm Little Riding Hood, yes I am!"

"It seems so much that a little girl like you should be carrying such a heavy basket. Perhaps I could help you," said the big wolf, grinning mischievously.

"That's okay, Wolf. I am strong. I can carry it by myself. Granny's house is only a quarter mile ahead. Thank you." And Little Riding Hood skipped in the direction of her grandmother's house.

But the crafty and cunning wolf showed Little Riding Hood a beautiful bouquet of blossoms. "Wouldn't your grandmother love these flowers?" he asked.

Little Riding Hood answered, "You are right. I think Granny would love some of these flowers to set on the table."

So the wolf began to bargain. "I'll give you these beautiful flowers in exchange for your pretty riding hood. My ears are always exposed and your riding hood would keep them warm."

The wolf made puppy eyes at Little Riding Hood, and she said, "Very well." So she traded her hood for the flowers and tromped deeper into the woods, while the cunning wolf dashed ahead to her grandmother's house. When he arrived at Granny's house, he knocked on the door.

"Who is it?" yelled Granny.

"It's me, Little Riding Hood. I've come to deliver a gift," answered the wolf, trying to disguise his voice.

"Freshly baked bread and homemade jam
I'm Little Riding Hood, yes I am!"

"Then come on in, Little Riding Hood. Granny has missed you."

The wolf opened the door and entered the house. As soon as Granny saw him, she bolted out of bed and ran to the door. But it was too late. The big wolf caught her and gobbled her down in one gulp. He then put on her apron and her bonnet and hopped into bed, waiting for Little Riding Hood.

By and by, Little Riding Hood knocked on the door.

"Who is it?" yelled the wolf, disguising his voice to sound like Granny.

"It's me, Little Riding Hood. I've come to deliver a gift," answered Little Riding Hood.

"Freshly baked bread and homemade jam
I'm Little Riding Hood, yes I am!"

"Then come on in, Little Riding Hood. Granny has missed you."

Little Riding Hood opened the door and entered the house, setting the basket and a handful of flowers on the table. Little Riding Hood saw who she thought was Granny lying in bed.

She approached the bed and said, "Granny what big ears you have."

The wolf answered, "The better to hear you with, my dear."

"And Granny, what big eyes you have."

The wolf answered, "The better to see you with, my dear."

"And Granny, what a big nose you have!"

The wolf answered, "The better to smell you with, my dear."

"And Granny, what big TEETH you have!"

The wolf answered, "The better to EAT you with, my dear!"

The words were scarcely out of his mouth when he sprang up out of bed, chasing Little Riding Hood. But she was quick, quick, quick. She gave the wolf a good chase and finally bounded out the door. The wolf did not tire easily; he followed her out as Little Riding Hood cried, "Help! Help!"

It just so happened that a nearby woodsman heard Little Riding Hood's cries for help. He ran to Little Riding Hood and just in the nick of time, he caught the wolf with his bare hands, just before the wolf caught Little Riding Hood. With his strong arms, he knocked that wolf silly. Before you know it, the woodsman reached down into the wolf's mouth and pulled out Granny. Then he took that puny old wolf and threw him deep into the woods. Granny was a little shaken up but none the worse for the wear. And believe me, the wolf never bothered any of them again.

Granny and Little Riding Hood invited the woodsman over to share a little gift.

"Freshly baked bread and homemade jam
I'm Little Riding Hood, yes I am!"

Deep, deep, way deep in the woods, a girl, a Granny, and a woodsman ate, drank, and rejoiced into the night.

And that my friends is the very, very end.

Maria's Dance
A Tear and Twist Tale

Supplies Needed:
- 1 7 x 7" sheet of stiff tissue paper
- Drinking straw
- Glass of water

Note from Dianne:
I learned how to make Maria when I was a little girl living in southern Spain. Flamenco dancing is part of the culture. A family friend taught me how to turn a napkin into a dancing flamenco girl. Since the napkins in Spain are much stiffer than traditional American napkins, I use stiff tissue paper instead of a napkin. The best part about Maria is making her dance. At the end of the story, add a couple drops of water to her arms using a drinking straw. Her arms will turn as if she is dancing flamenco. Be sure to have several tissue squares prepared. The kids will ask you to repeat it over and over . . .

Story:
Maria was tired of everyone telling her she was too young to dance. All her life, she had been taught to dance but yet, they would not let her perform at *la feria*, the fair.

[*Start with a 7 x 7" square of stiff tissue paper.*]

One day, Maria's *Abuela* (grandmother) came into her room. "Maria," she said, "I have *una sorpresa* for you. A surprise!"

[*Roll the tissue paper into a cylinder about 2 inches in diameter.*]

Her grandmother had a huge box in her arms. She lifted the lid of the box and inside the box was the most beautiful flamenco dress Maria had ever seen. It was red with white polka dots. It was trimmed in white lace with a huge poufy skirt. It was everything Maria had dreamed it would be.

[*Pinch the middle of the cylinder and twist it a couple of times, creating two bells.*]

"You must get ready," *Abuela* said. "You are going to dance at *la feria* tonight!"

Maria hugged *Abuela*. She was so excited! She put on her dress and placed a big rose in her hair. Tonight was her big debut!

[*On one side of the twist, tear the bell into three equal sections.*]

Maria warmed up her arms and practiced her steps. She couldn't wait to dance!

[*Twist the right and left sides into arms. The middle section becomes the head. Twist a ponytail on Maria's head.*]

That night, Maria stepped on stage and danced with all her heart. When she was finished, the crowd applauded wildly. *Abuela* looked at her from the audience with a proud smile. Maria now felt like a real flamenco dancer!

[*Add a couple of drops of water to her arms using a drinking straw. Her arms will turn as if she is dancing flamenco.*]

The Möbius Brothers' Circus
A Möbius Strip Tale

Supplies Needed:
- 1 sheet of colored construction paper
- Tape
- Scissors

Note from Dianne:

Möbius strips are fun in a story time and a great science tie-in. Upper elementary-aged children will have fun creating Möbius strips and trying to figure them out. A kind librarian in Missouri taught me a story with Möbius strips that was passed to her from her grandmother. It was about a circus. While I forgot the story, I still remember the Möbius strips. Here is my ode to her Möbius circus story.

Story:

Jenevieve was so excited to go to the circus. She couldn't wait to see all the acts!

[*Start with a sheet of colored construction paper in the landscape orientation.*]

She was going to the Möbius Brothers' Circus!

[*Fold the construction paper in half from top to bottom and half again, from top to bottom into quarters.*]

There would be acrobats, a motorcycle daredevil, clowns, and tigers!

[*Cut along the creases, creating four strips. You will use three of the strips.*]

Jenevieve held her mother's hand, and they walked inside the three-ring circus.

[*With the first strip, create a loop and tape it closed.*]

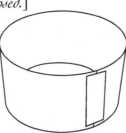

They sat down, and the first amazing act had trained tigers. The ringmaster had the tigers jump through two fire-covered hoops!

[*Cut the loop down the center.*]

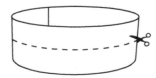

[*You will end up with two separate rings.*]

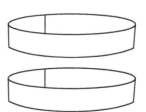

Then the clowns came out and cut up. They drove around the ring beeping their horns and making people laugh.

[*With the second strip, create a loop, giving it a half turn before attaching the ends together.*]

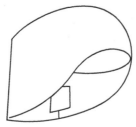

[*Cut the loop down the center all the way around.*]

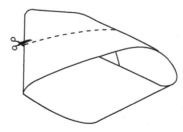

Next, an amazing motorcycle daredevil came out. He rode his motorcycle around a track that even had him upside down! Jenevieve squealed with delight!

[*You will end up with a loop that is twice the size of the original.*]

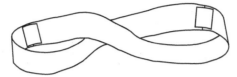

Elephants came out, and ladies twisted on ribbons hanging from the ceiling.

[*With the third strip, give the strip a full turn and then attach the ends together with tape.*]

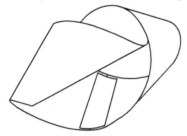

Then it was time for the finale . . . the acrobatic acts. Jenevieve held her breath as the tightrope walker balanced on a long wire.

[*Cut the loop down the middle all the way around.*]

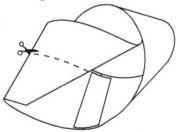

But the highlight of the circus was seeing the acrobats fly through the air. They linked together and flew through the air like birds.

[*You will end up with two interlocking loops. Hold them up and swing them from side to side like acrobats in the air.*]

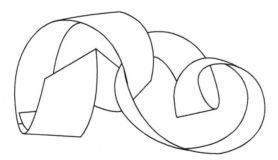

It was a great day. Jenevieve loved the circus. She couldn't wait to go again!

The Mouse's Wedding — Japan
A Paper Plate Cutting Tale

Supplies Needed:
- 5 large paper plates
- Marker
- Scissors

Note from Dianne:

I used this same story in *Handmade Tales* using handkerchiefs. In *Kamishibai Story Theater*, it was a great paper drama tale. I love this story because it is so versatile and lends itself to a variety of storytelling methods. Now here is one with paper plates!

Paper Plate Hat Basic Instructions:

1. Fold a large paper plate in half.

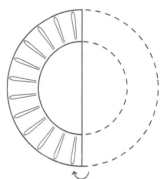

2. Cut a 1 inch circular strip around the inner edge of the paper plate. Leave the inner circle attached.

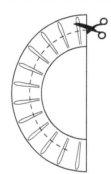

3. The inner circle can then be cut into different shapes.

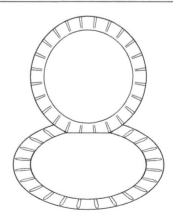

4. Place the ridged circle on your head.
   This is the hat's rim. The inner circle stands
   up on the forehead. Draw faces on your characters.

5. Make all of the paper plate story hats
   ahead of time for use when telling the story.

Story:

Long ago, there lived a rich mouse who had a beautiful daughter. His daughter had a handsome but poor suitor. The poor mouse wanted to marry the beautiful daughter, but Father Mouse wanted his daughter to marry the mightiest creature in the world.

Father Mouse spoke to his wife. "Wife, our daughter has a common mouse for a suitor. But I cannot let my daughter marry unless she marries the mightiest creature in the world. Everyone knows the mightiest one is Mr. Sun."

Mother Mouse said, "Perhaps you should see him and ask him to marry our daughter." Father Mouse thought it was a good idea and set off to see the sun.

[*Place sun hat on your head.*]

When he arrived, he bowed. "Good day, Mr. Sun. I want my daughter to marry the mightiest creature in the world. Since you bring light to the world, you must be the mightiest."

The Sun smiled, "I am flattered, but I am afraid I am not the mightiest. When Mr. Cloud passes by, he covers my face, therefore, he must be the mightiest."

Father Mouse thanked the Sun and continued on his journey.

[*Place cloud hat on your head.*]

When he found the Cloud, he bowed. "Good Day, Mr. Cloud. I want my daughter to marry the mightiest creature in the world. Since you cover Mr. Sun, you must be the mightiest."

The Cloud smiled, "I am flattered, but I am afraid I am not the mightiest. When Mr. Wind comes near, he blows me across the sky, therefore, he must be the mightiest."

Father Mouse thanked the Cloud and continued on his journey.

[*Place wind hat on your head.*]

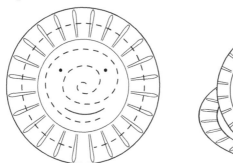

When he found the Wind, he bowed. "Good Day, Mr. Wind. I want my daughter to marry the mightiest creature in the world. Since you blow Mr. Cloud across the sky, you must be the mightiest."

The Wind smiled, "I am flattered, but I am afraid I am not the mightiest. When I approach Mr. Wall, he stops me in my tracks, therefore, he must be the mightiest."

Father Mouse thanked the Wind and continued on his journey.

[*Place wall hat on your head.*]

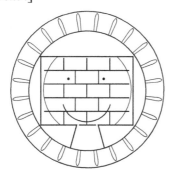
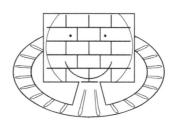

When he found the Wall, he bowed. "Good Day, Mr. Wall. I want my daughter to marry the mightiest creature in the world. Since you stop Mr. Wind in his tracks, you must be the mightiest."

The Wall smiled, "I am flattered, but I am afraid I am not the mightiest. Do you see that hole in me? That hole is made by the mightiest creature around. He has the power to chew right through me!"

Father Mouse asked, "Honorable Mr. Wall, what creature has that kind of power?"

The Wall laughed. "Why, it's you, the mouse! You must be the mightiest creature in the world!"

[*Place mouse hat on your head*.]

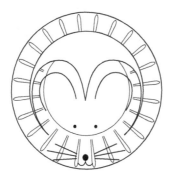 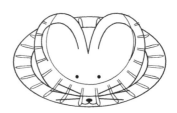

Father Mouse was surprised. He thanked the Wall and journeyed home. He told his daughter to prepare for a wedding! Father Mouse discovered that the mightiest creature in the world was not the sun, the mightiest creature in the world was not the cloud, the mightiest creature in the world was not the wind, the mightiest creature in the world was not the wall. The mightiest creature in the world turned out to be a common . . . [*Allow audience to chime in the answer as you point to the mouse.*] mouse!

The mouse and the beautiful daughter were married. And they lived . . . mousily ever after!

The Naughty (Knotty) Bunny
A Handkerchief Tale

Supplies Needed:
- 1 large bandana
- 3 rubber bands

Note from Dianne:
Use the bunny as a puppet for this story. You can create munching motions with your free hand as you tell the story. The children will love the audience participation in this story. At the end of the story, when you say, "It's time to stop." Lower your voice and the audience will, too. They will even fill in the "stop" if you do a dramatic pause before the word.

Bunny Instructions:
1. Use a large bandana.

2. Fold bandana in half, creating a triangle.

3. On each side of the triangle, tie a small knot. These will become his arms.

4. Tie a large knot at the top of the triangle leaving about 2 inches of excess bandana sticking up. The knot is the bunny's head. The excess fabric, when separated, becomes his ears.

5. Tie a rubber band around the bunny's middle.

6. On the bottom of the bunny, gather the fabric and tie rubber bands around each side, creating feet.

7. Insert finger into back of head to create a bunny puppet.

Story:
There was once a little bunny who was really bad
He was eating all the cabbage that the farmer had

Gobble, gobble, crunch
Munch, munch, munch
Gobble, gobble, crunch
Munch, munch, munch

Naughty Bunny ate everything he could
Because that cabbage tasted oh so good!

Gobble, gobble, crunch
Munch, munch, munch
Gobble, gobble, crunch
Munch, munch, munch

He ate all the carrots, nibbled all the peas
Naughty Bunny ate whatever he pleased

Gobble, gobble, crunch
Munch, munch, munch
Gobble, gobble, crunch
Munch, munch, munch

Gone was the lettuce, gone were the beans
Gone was the garden with yummy greens!

Gobble, gobble, crunch
Munch, munch, munch
Gobble, gobble, crunch
Munch, munch, munch

The farmer didn't think it was very funny
To fill the hungry tummy of Naughty Bunny

Gobble, gobble, crunch
Munch, munch, munch
Gobble, gobble, crunch
Munch, munch, munch

So he put up a fence and said, "Stay out!
You won't eat the cabbage for my sauerkraut!"

Gobble, gobble, crunch
Munch, munch, munch
Gobble, gobble, crunch
Munch, munch, munch

So little Naughty Bunny had to go away
I guess he'll have to eat another day!

Hippy, hippy, hop
It's time to stop!

Patty's Tale
A Paper Accordion Tale

Supplies Needed:
- 3 sheets of 8 ½ x 11" white copy paper
- Glue stick or double-stick tape
- Pencil
- Black marker

Note from Dianne:

I love accordion books. I bought one in Singapore called *HenSparrow Turns Purple* that was stunning, and I love the way it slowly reveals each page through its folds. It inspired me to create this simple story using the same technique. Dinosaurs are a childhood favorite, and Patty (short for "Apatosaurus") is a crowd pleaser.

Apatosaurus Instructions:

1. Start with three sheets of 8 ½ x 11" paper in the landscape orientation. Stack them on top of each other.

2. Fold the sheets in half from side to side.

3. Fold the top three layers to the left side, creating an accordion pleat.

4. Fold the remaining layers down, creating another accordion pleat.

5. Using a glue stick or double-stick tape, attach the three accordion sheets together, laying one panel over another. There will be ten panels.

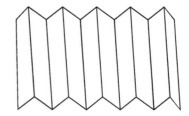

6. Stretch out the accordion and draw an Apatosaurus with pencil. The Apatosaurus should be facing right. Trace over it with black marker.

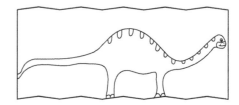

Story:
Perry was walking in the forest along the river one day.

[*Reveal panel one.*]

He realized there was something unusual in the area. He continued following the river.

[*Reveal panels two and three.*]

He reached an area where the river flowed into a lake. The water flowed in different directions and he didn't know which way to go. He trusted his gut feeling and followed along the lake's shore.

[*Reveal panels four and five.*]

That was when Perry thought he spotted something BIG with TEETH! He was nervous but curious even more, so he journeyed onward.

[*Reveal panels six and seven.*]

Oh my gosh! Could it be a long . . . snake?! Perry perished the thought. He continued on.

[*Reveal panels eight and nine.*]

Perry was glad that he trusted himself and continued his journey, because he couldn't believe what he saw. It wasn't a scary beast with big teeth or a slithering creature with a venomous bite. Instead, a friendly face smiled at him.

[*Reveal panel ten.*]

It was an Apatosaurus. She introduced herself as "Patty." Well, Patty and Perry began taking LOOOOOONG walks through the forest. They became the very best of friends. And that's the end of that tale . . .

[*Reveal all panels and entire dinosaur.*]

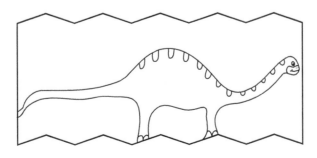

Puppy and Bunny
A Towel Folding Tale

Supplies Needed:
- 2 colored washcloths
- Rubber bands
- Googly eyes
- Hole-punched pink construction paper nose
- Hole-punched black construction paper nose

Note from Dianne:
I went on a cruise and was so inspired by the towel folding that I took a class! I made friends with one of the instructors and had my own private tutor. It was so much fun! The characters in this story are made of washcloths. They both use the same basic folds but a little adjusting of the rubber band and the cloth makes them completely different animals. Use them as finger puppets and you will surely get lots of "awwws" from your audience!

Folding Instructions:
1. Start with a washcloth in the diamond orientation.

2. Fold washcloth in half from bottom to top, creating a triangle.

3. Roll triangle from bottom to top, forming a tight cylinder.

4. Fold roll in half.

5. With hole at the top of the roll facing you,
   fold the two bottom rolls up so that two inches
   of cloth extend above the top of the roll.
   Wrap a rubber band around the middle, securing it.
   Right now, you have a duck.

6. Tuck beak inside and pull face down. Adjust the ears.
   You have a bunny.

7. (Back view of dog) To make puppy, pull ears forward
   and use one rubber band loop from the back to secure
   the ears.

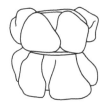

8. Puppy's front

9. Puppy and Bunny together. Decorate them with
   googly eyes or stickers and add hole-punched noses,
   black for puppy and pink for Bunny.

Story:
Puppy was happy in his little world. He had everything he wanted: a loving master, a favorite ball, and a doghouse in the backyard.

[*Place Puppy on your index finger by inserting your finger into the rubber band on his backside.*]

At least he thought he had everything he wanted. There was one thing Puppy didn't have . . . someone to play with.

[*Move Puppy around as though he is in his backyard.*]

One day, it was storming, and Puppy had to retreat inside his doghouse. Thunder rolled and he curled in the corner whimpering. He was scared.

[*You can create a "doghouse" out of a small milk carton or even a paper lunch bag if you want.*]

Just as lightning cracked across the sky, a white ball of fur shot into the doghouse. Puppy had an intruder!

[*Don't introduce Bunny just yet.*]

Puppy began barking at the intruder.

"Yap, yap, yippity yap
Yap, yap, yippity yap!"

The little ball of fur was Bunny. He was frightened by the storm and ran for shelter. Puppy's doghouse looked like a good place to hide. Bunny shivered. Clearly, this puppy was not friendly!

[*Bring out Bunny and place him on your opposite index finger.*]

Puppy stared at Bunny. The white ball of fur seemed scared. Puppy wagged his tail and licked Bunny's face.

[*Have Puppy "lick" Bunny and make slurping sounds.*]

Bunny smiled. This puppy was friendly after all. He hopped around the doghouse, and Puppy rolled around. Puppy yapped and Bunny hopped.

"Yap, yap, yippity yap
Hop, hop, hippity, hop
Yap, yap, yippity yap!
Hop, hop, hippity, hop!"

[*Have the children join in with you.*]

Soon, the storm was over. Puppy and Bunny ventured into the yard. Puppy yapped and Bunny hopped.

"Yap, yap, yippity yap
Hop, hop, hippity, hop
Yap, yap, yippity yap!
Hop, hop, hippity, hop!"

[*Have the children join in with you.*]

Finally, Puppy had a new play pal. Every day Bunny came over to keep Puppy company. Puppy yapped and Bunny hopped.

"Yap, yap, yippity yap
Hop, hop, hippity, hop
Yap, yap, yippity yap!
Hop, hop, hippity, hop!"

They became good friends and were always there to comfort each other when a thunderstorm rolled through.

"Yap, yap, yippity yap
That's the end of that!"

Shine So Bright
A String Tale

Supplies Needed:
- 1 4 ft. loop of string

Note from Dianne:
I learned this string figure from string figure master David Titus. I love this star because it's so easy once you learn it and the children LOVE it. I wrote a short poem to go with the star that is great to use in the classroom and in the library. Practice making the star. Once you have mastered it, recite the poem as you are forming the star. The kids will be in awe of you.

String Star Instructions:
1. Double the string and loop it around your palm.

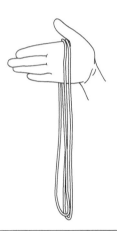

2. Place string behind pinky, over palm, and behind thumb.

From *Handmade Tales 2: More Stories to Make and Take* by Dianne de Las Casas. Santa Barbara, CA: Libraries Unlimited. Copyright © 2013.

3. Loop the other end around the index finger of
   your opposite hand.

4. At the top of the triangle, bring thumb
   and pinky together.

5. Reach across and insert the thumb and pinky over
   the top of string across palm of opposite hand.

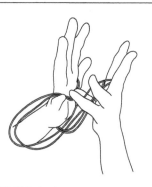

6. Pull thumb and pinky back.

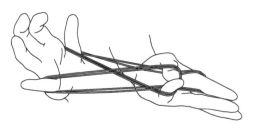

7. Open thumb and pinky and you have a star.

Story:
If you try with all your might
You will shine; shine so bright
You are here; you've come so far
Because you are . . .

   A reading star!

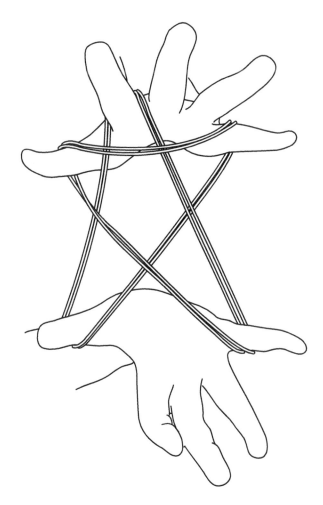

Story Spinner Game
A Fold and Spin Activity

Supplies Needed:
- 1 4 x 6" index card
- Scissors
- Markers
- Pen

Note from Dianne:

Spinners are popular playground activities in elementary schools. Rather than confiscate them from the children, I have chosen to turn them into an educational story spinner game. Playing the game allows them to have fun with their beloved spinners while improving their storytelling skills and increasing their oral communication abilities.

Story Spinner Instructions:
1. Fold 4 x 6" card in half lengthwise.

2. Following the crease, cut the card in half.

3. Fold the top corners to the opposite edge creating triangles on the top and bottom of each strip.

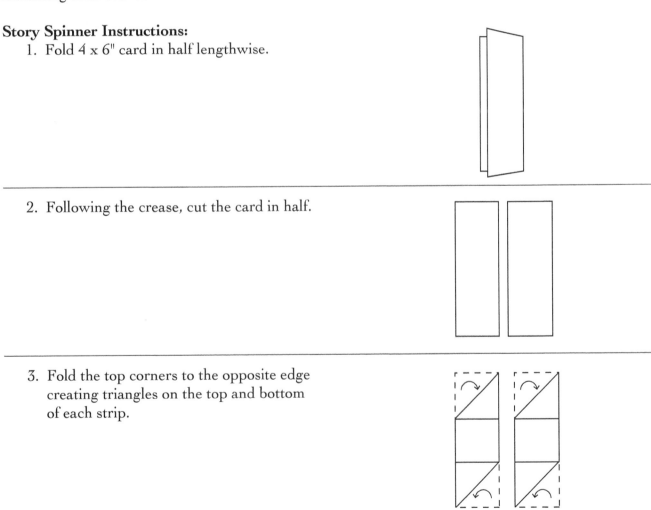

4. Place one folded strip on top of the other,
   forming a star.

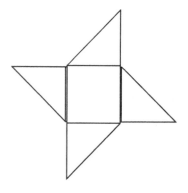

5. Fold the top point down, creating the beginning
   of a square.

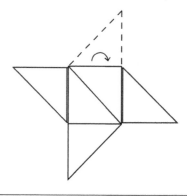

6. Fold the right point over the top point.

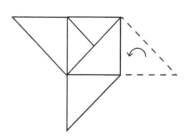

7. Fold the bottom point up, over the right point.

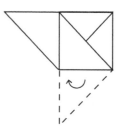

8. Fold the left point over the bottom point and
   tuck into the slot at the top

9. Color each triangle a different color.

10. Write a story opening under each triangle.

---

11. Write a story prompt under the folded triangle,
    which opens up into a square.

Story Openings:
1. Once upon a time . . .
2. Long, long ago . . .
3. In the olden days . . .
4. In a land far away . . .
5. In times of magic . . .
6. Once there was and once there wasn't . . .
7. Twice upon a time . . .
8. In times of ancient things . . .

Story Prompts:
1. There was once an ugly princess . . .
2. There was once a lazy dragon . . .
3. There was once a booger-picking ogre . . .
4. There was once a farting giant . . .
5. There was once a sneezing fairy . . .
6. There was once a wacky witch . . .
7. There was once a fearsome monster . . .
8. There was once a laughing troll . . .

Game Instructions:
1. There can be two to six players.
2. A player is chosen to go first, and the game continues clockwise.
3. The story spinner is spun.
4. Player one lifts the flap of whatever color stops in front of him/her. If the spinner stops at the
   point, the player lifts the flap of the color of his/her choice. It is read aloud.

5. Player one spins one more time and lifts the flap twice of whatever color stops in front of him/her (i.e., Twice upon a time . . . there was a sneezing fairy who could not keep her flying fairy dust about her. She kept sneezing it onto animals and people. Soon, everyone began flying . . .).

6. The player continues until the story is complete, using at least six to eight sentences to tell the story.

7. Alternatively, the game can be played with player one starting a round-robin story to which everyone in the group contributes.

Tina's Misadventure

A Paper Bag Tear and Tell Tale

Supplies Needed:
- 2 small brown paper lunch bags

Note from Dianne:
The beauty of this story is in the tearing. It's fun to watch each piece of the paper bag transform into something unexpected. Every single part of both paper bags is used. Nothing is wasted in this tale.

Story:
Tina didn't always listen to her mom. Her mother warned her never to walk through the forest alone, but Tina didn't listen. She decided that she was bored and wanted an adventure! Unfortunately, as she was walking through the forest, she came across a . . . snake!

[Start with a brown lunch bag with the bottom facing left.]

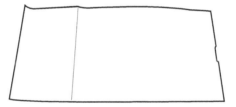

[Tear off a 1 inch strip from the top of the paper bag.]

[Tear apart the loop. Twist and crumple 1 inch strip to form snake.]

Tina's heart stopped. What was she going to do? Fortunately, she saw a tree nearby and decided to climb the tree. Quickly, she jumped up the tree and began climbing her way to the top. Unfortunately, snakes can climb, too, and it began following her!

[Tear off a 3 inch wide strip from the remaining paper bag.]

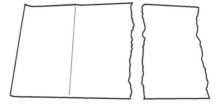

[Tear apart the loop and twist and tear to form a tree.]

Tina had to react quickly. Fortunately, there was a vine on the tree. Tina grabbed the vine and swung to the next tree. She used vines to swing from tree to tree until she was far away from the snake!

[Tear off a 1 inch strip from the remaining paper bag.]

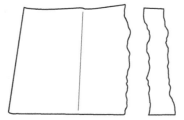

[Twist 1 inch strip into a vine.]

At the top of the tall tree she could see something in the distance. Could it be?! It was! Tina saw a house. It had a door, and it had a window.

[*Use remainder of bag to form the base of the house. Tear a door and window.*]

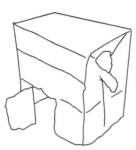

But it was no ordinary house. No sirree! It was the house of Tina's grandma! The door was unlocked, and the window was open. It seemed that Tina's grandma was expecting company.

[*Use another brown lunch bag and tear 7 to 8 inches off.*]

[*Fold the strip in half to form the roof.*]

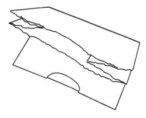

[*Place the roof on top of the house base.*]

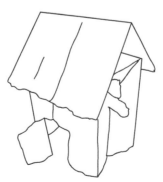

Tina climbed down from the tree and ran to her grandma's house. Grandma wrapped her loving arms around Tina and gave her a big hug and a big bowl of hot porridge.

[*Use remaining paper bag to form a bowl. Cuff edge and shape into a circle.*]

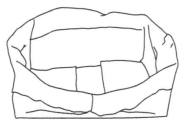

Tina ate up all of the porridge. From that time on, she never ventured into the forest alone again!

The Tortoise and The Hare
A Paper Plate and Twine Tale

Supplies Needed:
- 2 large paper plates
- 1 straw
- Tape
- Twine
- Black marker

Note from Dianne:
Children love racing the tortoise and hare. They can either make their own tortoise and hare, or take turns racing the animals on the string. Each race could have a different outcome depending on the children.

Hare Directions:
1. Cut a large paper plate in half. One half will be the hare's body.

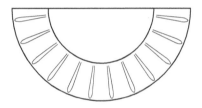

2. Using the other half of the paper plate, cut a half circle using the inner circle line as a guide. This will be the hare's head.

3. Cut leftover outer ridge of the plate in half. These will become the hare's ears.

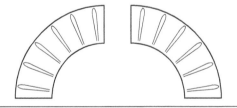

4. Using tape, attach the head to the top of the straight edge of the paper plate half.

5. Tape the ears to the head.

6. Using a marker, draw the inside of the ears, a face, legs, and a cotton tail.

7. Cut the straw in half and tape it to the back of the top of the head.

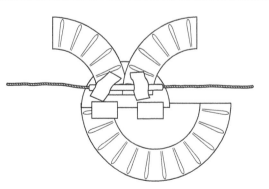

From *Handmade Tales 2: More Stories to Make and Take* by Dianne de Las Casas. Santa Barbara, CA: Libraries Unlimited. Copyright © 2013.

8. Thread 4 yards of twine through it.

Tortoise Directions:

1. Cut the inner circle out of a large paper plate.
   This will become the tortoise's body.

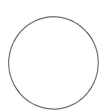

2. Using one quarter of the outer ridge of the paper plate,
   cut out a head, four legs, and a triangular tail.

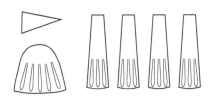

3. Using tape, attach the head to one side of the circle.
   Attach the tail to the opposite side of the circle.

4. Tape the legs to the bottom of the circle.

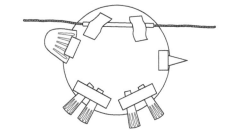

5. Using a marker, draw the tortoise's face and shell.

6. Use the other half of the straw and tape it to the back
   of the top of the tortoise shell.

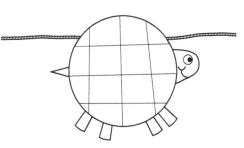

7. Thread 4 yards of twine through it.

Race Instructions:

1. The race will require at least two to four people.
2. Hold each end of the strings the same distance apart.
3. Place the tortoise and the hare in the same position at the beginning of the race. Hare and
   tortoise should face the same direction.
4. To move the animals, the person at the beginning of the race needs to lift the string while the
   person on the other end keeps the string stationary. The animals will slide forward.
5. To control how much the tortoise and the hare move forward, the person at the end of the race
   can lift the string to prevent forward movement.

Story:
From a far-off land neither here nor there
I bring you the fable of the Tortoise and the Hare

Hare was very conceited and thought that he was the most handsome animal in all of the forest. He would often gaze into the mirror and say, "I am so handsome. Look at my lovely long ears, my pretty pink nose, and my beautiful buck teeth!" He also thought that he was the fastest animal in all of the forest.

One day, Hare overheard a group of turtles talking. They said, "Cousin Tortoise has never lost a race. He always wins!"

"Ha!" scoffed Hare, "we'll see about that!" He marched over to the group of turtles and said, "Everyone knows that I am the fastest animal in all of the forest. Tell your cousin Tortoise that I challenge him to a race!"

The next day, Tortoise met Hare in the clearing. He said, "Hello, I am Tortoise. Are you ready to race?"

Hare answered with a laugh, "Of course I am, because I am the fastest animal in all of the forest. Prepare to eat my dust!"

Tortoise and Hare lined up. Raccoon held her tail up in the air and said, "On your mark, ready, ready, go!"

Hare took off and left Tortoise in a cloud of dust. Meanwhile . . .

Tortoise never wavered from the race
He kept on going at a steady pace

[*Start the race of the tortoise and the hare on the strings, stopping about a quarter of the way on the strings.*]

Hare looked behind and saw that he was far ahead of Tortoise. He decided he had time for a little break. So he stopped by the side of the road and pulled out his mirror. He said, "Just look at me. So handsome. Not a hair out of place." As Hare admired himself, he saw another reflection in the mirror. It was . . . Tortoise! You see . . .

Tortoise never wavered from the race
He kept on going at a steady pace

[*Continue the race of the tortoise and the hare on the strings, stopping about another quarter of the way on the strings.*]

Hare yelled, "Oh no! I gotta go!" And he took off faster than a speeding bullet. Hare looked behind and saw that he was way ahead of Tortoise. He decided that he had time for a little snack. So he stopped and ordered fries and a strawberry shake. He was sipping his shake when he saw . . . Tortoise! You see . . .

Tortoise never wavered from the race
He kept on going at a steady pace

[*Continue the race of the tortoise and the hare on the strings, stopping about another quarter of the way on the strings.*]

Hare yelled, "Oh no! I gotta go!" and he took off faster than a tornado. Hare ran for a while. Then he looked behind and saw that he was way, way ahead of Tortoise. There was no sign of Tortoise at all! Hare decided that he had time for a little . . . nap. He sat down by the side of the road, under the shade of a tall tree and began to snooze (snoring sounds). Meanwhile . . .

Tortoise never wavered from the race
He kept on going at a steady pace

[*Continue the race of the tortoise and the hare on the strings, ending the race with the tortoise winning.*]

Hare woke up just in time to see Tortoise approaching the finish line. Hare yelled, "Oh no! I gotta go!" and he took off faster than lightning. But it was too late. Although Hare was close behind, Tortoise crossed the finish line. Tortoise won the race by just a . . . hare! You see . . .

Tortoise never wavered from the race
He kept on going at a steady pace

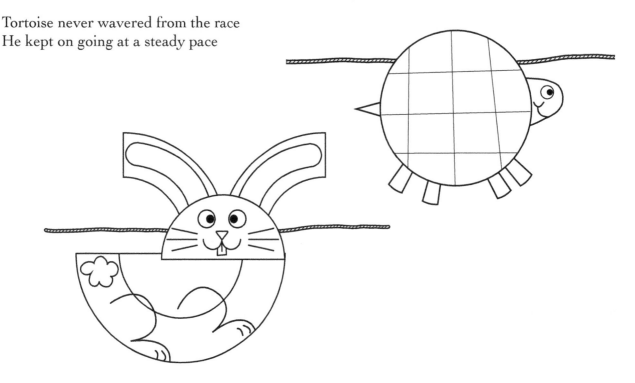

The Wide Mouth Frog
A Towel Folding Tale

Supplies Needed:
- 1 large green bath towel
- 2 large, sticky googly eyes or large eye stickers

Note from Dianne:
A tale from North America, the most charming version of this story was taught to me by author, storyteller, and musician Dan Keding. Dan used both of his hands to form the head of the frog, much to the delight of his audience. In this version, the frog is created with a green large bath towel. Exaggerate the dialogue of the frog, making him loud as well as wide. I have added more hand motions to portray the other characters in the story.

Towel Frog Instructions:
1. You will need a large bath towel.

2. With the towel in portrait position, fold it in half from top to bottom.

3. Fold the towel in half again from top to bottom.

4. Fold the top right corner to the bottom edge of the towel, forming a triangle. Do the same with the top left corner.

---

5. Fold both sides of the towel together, standing it up.

---

6. Push the top of the towel down, forming the frog's head. The bottoms of the towel on each side become his feet.

---

7. Add googly eyes or eye stickers to the top of his head.

Story:
The Wide Mouth Frog lived in a pond. [*Form the towel frog.*] One day, he decided to venture out to see the wide, wide world.

As he hopped along, he came upon a red animal flapping her wings. [*Extend arms out and flap.*]

The Wide Mouth Frog said, "HELLO! Who are you and what do you eat?"

The animal [*flap arms*] said, "I am a . . . [*Pause slightly to allow audience to chime in answer.*] bird. And I eat wet, wiggly worms. [*Make a wiggly worm by moving index finger back and forth.*]

The Wide Mouth Frog said, "OH! That's nice." And he hopped on.

As he hopped along, he came upon a black and white animal swishing her tail back and forth. [*Wave backside from side to side. This will get a laugh from the audience.*]

The Wide Mouth Frog said, "HELLO! Who are you and what do you eat?"

The animal [*Swish tail.*] said, "Mooooooo. I am a . . . [*Pause slightly to allow audience to chime in answer.*] cow. And I eat great, green grass." [*Make grass by motioning both hands back and forth.*]

The Wide Mouth Frog said, "OH! That's nice." And he hopped on.

As he hopped along, he came upon a tall, furry brown animal with big claws and sharp teeth. [*Hold up both hands and bend fingers to make claws. Scrunch up face to look mean.*]

The Wide Mouth Frog said, "HELLO! Who are you and what do you eat?"

The animal [*Snarl and make clawing motion.*] said, "Grrrrrrrrowl. I am a . . . [*Pause slightly to allow audience to chime in answer.*] bear. And I eat sweet, sticky honey." [*Wipe chin with both hands and make slurping sounds.*]

The Wide Mouth Frog said, "OH! That's nice." And he hopped on.

As he hopped along, he came upon a long green animal with a big jaw and sharp teeth. [*Elongate arms and put hands together, opening and closing hands to make snapping sounds.*]

The Wide Mouth Frog said, "HELLO! Who are you and what do you eat?"

The animal [*Clap hands together loudly.*] said, "Snap. I am an . . . [*Pause slightly to allow audience to chime in answer.*] ALLIGATOR. And I eat . . . wide mouth frogs." [*Make frog shake with fear.*]

The Wide Mouth Frog said, "OH NO!" And he hopped on. From that time on, the Wide Mouth Frog never again wandered in the wide, wide world.

Source Notes

"3-2-1 . . . Rudolph!" is an original story. I came up with the story for a holiday program for Janet Perez at St. Bernard Parish Library, Louisiana. It was so much fun to create a story using numbers, very similar to my story "Catching a Pest in 7 Steps" in *Handmade Tales: Stories to Make and Take*.

"3-2-1 . . . Santa!" is an original story. Again, I created the story for a holiday program for Janet Perez at St. Bernard Parish Library, Louisiana.

"Amy's Love" is an original story. I love Möbius strips and wanted to create a story using them. During my research on the Internet, I came across a YouTube video of a couple folding a Möbius heart. It took a couple of tries but I learned it! http://www.youtube.com/watch?v=o2hqM8BgjK0

"Baby J" is an original story. My niece Camrynn taught me how to make the jacket baby. It is very popular on playgrounds and would make a great prop for any story with a baby in it.

"BINGO" is a popular children's song in the public domain. I love draw and tell tales that use letters to form the pictures. I experimented (MANY times) to come up with the face of a dog using the letters B-I-N-G-O. It's fun to draw as the kids are singing the song.

"The Captain's Shirt" is an adaptation of a story I heard as a little girl. It is a popular scout tale. I gave the story a bit more suspense and a ghostly ending, which I think makes more sense of "the captain's shirt."

"Cassidy's Bud" is an original story. I love napkin folding and in the original *Handmade Tales*, I included a story with napkin-folding called "The Snooks Family." I learned how to fold the napkin from a book called *Classic Napkin Folds* by Rick Beech (New York: Metro Books, 2010).

"Edward's Pet" is an original story. A Pre-K teacher taught me how to fold the elephant. I paired the elephant with an original story. It's so much fun for the kids to fold along with you.

"Fairy-Tale Flashcards" is an original game. I was inspired by an Asian fan folding technique to create the flashcards. Children need more exposure to fairy tales and folktales and this is a fun game to familiarize them with those stories.

"The Frog Jumping Jamboree" is an original story. I have been teaching children how to create this hopping origami frog for years. Rayne, Louisiana, is called the Frog Capital of the World. Every year, they hold a frog jumping and racing contest. Every time I drove by Rayne, I said I wanted to write a frog jumping story. Well, here it is, combining my love of origami with a frog jumping jamboree.

"George's Surprise" is an original story. I have known how to make the origami puppy for years and have always wanted to pair it with a story. Children love the reveal of the dog at the end of this tale.

"The Grumpy Leprechaun" is an original story. One year, I needed to create a St. Patrick's Day craft. I thought a paper plate would make a great shamrock. Once I perfected the shamrock, I created the story to go with it.

"Jack and the Beanstalk" was adapted from "Jack and the Beanstalk" in *The Red Fairy Book*, edited by Andrew Lang (New York: MFJ Books, 1994, originally published in 1890), "Jack and the Beanstalk" in *Best-Loved Folktales of the World*, edited by Joanna Cole (New York: Anchor Books: 1982), and "Jack and the Beanstalk" in *English Fairy Tales* by Joseph Jacobs (New York: Alfred A. Knopf, 1993, first published in 1890). The technique of the roll tale was inspired by ancient Indian and Japanese roll tales.

"Little Riding Hood" was adapted from "The Little Red Riding Hood" in *The Blue Fairy Book*, edited by Andrew Lang (New York: MJF Books, 1889), "Little Red Riding Hood" in *Best-Loved Folktales of the World*, edited by Joanna Cole (New York: Anchor Books, 1982), and "Little Red Riding Hood" in *The Everything Fairy Tales Book* by Amy Peters (Avon, MA: Adams Media Corporation, 2001).

"Maria's Dance" is an original story. I learned how to make Maria when I was a little girl living in southern Spain. Flamenco dancing is part of the culture. A family friend taught me how to turn a napkin into a dancing flamenco girl.

"The Möbius Brothers' Circus" is an original story. A kind librarian in Missouri taught me a story with Möbius strips that was passed to her from her grandmother. It was about a circus. While I forgot the story, I still remember the Möbius strips and created a new story.

"The Mouse's Wedding" was adapted from a Japanese Kamishibai play called "The Mouse's Wedding" by Seishi Horio (New York: Twinkle Tales for Kids, 1997), *The Mouse Bride* by Joy Crowley (New York: Scholastic, 1995), "The Beautiful Mouse Girl" in *Japanese Folktales* by James E. O'Donnell (Caldwell, Idaho: The Caxton Printers, 1958), and "Nezumi No Yomeiri" from Folk Legends of Japan website http://web-japan.org/kidsweb/folk.html. I made a basic hat from a paper plate and began experimenting with creating shapes out of the hat. My favorite is the mouse at the end of the tale.

"The Naughty Bunny" is an original story. I learned how to make the bunny out of a knotted bandana from a librarian at one of my workshops. The bunny was so cute I didn't unfold him for three years! LOL

"Patty's Tale" is an original story. I love accordion books. I bought one in Singapore called *HenSparrow Turns Purple* that was stunning, and I love the way it slowly reveals each page through its folds. It inspired me to create this simple story using the same technique but using each fold as an element of surprise. Dinosaurs are a childhood favorite, and Patty (short for "Apatosaurus") is a crowd-pleaser.

"Puppy and Bunny" is an original story. I went on a cruise and was so inspired by the towel folding that I took a class. I made friends with one of the instructors and had my own private tutor. It was so much fun! The characters in this story are made of washcloths. I learned the basic folds and through manipulating the washcloth, I found I could make several different animals including a duck, a pig, and a bear. I guess they'll have to make an appearance in another book! ;)

"Shine So Bright" is an original story. The star string figure was taught to me by string figure master David Titus (http://www.stringfigureministries.com). This is also where I order all of my professional strings for my workshops.

"Story Spinner Game" is an original game. Children from across the country have taught me how to make the spinner, an often-banned playground toy. My daughter Eliana helped me to perfect my folds. I wanted to make the spinner "educational," so I toyed with it until I came up with a game that makes it a fun story prompt that's great for the classroom and the library.

"Tina's Misadventure" is an original story. I love the idea of "tear and tell" tales. I began experimenting with a regular brown lunch bag. The funny thing is that the story came to me while simultaneously tearing the paper bags.

"The Tortoise and the Hare" is adapted from childhood memories of the story, "The Hare and the Tortoise" in *Aesop's Fables*, selected and adapted by Jack Zipes (New York: Penguin, 1992), "The Tortoise and the Hare" in *Troll Treasury of Animal Stories*, edited by John C. Miles (Mahwah, NJ: HarperCollins, 1991), and "The Hare and the Tortoise" in *Best-Loved Folktales of the World* edited by Joanna Cole (New York: Anchor Books, 1982). The story itself inspired the racing of the paper plate animals using string and straws.

"The Wide Mouth Frog" is adapted from a traditional tale called "The Wide Mouth Frog." Over the years, I have heard many storytellers tell this story. My favorite version, and the one that inspired my adaptation, is from storyteller and musician Dan Keding. In the original *Handmade Tales*, the frog is made with the hands. In this version, the frog is made with a towel, inspired by my cruise towel-folding class.

About the Author and the Illustrator

DIANNE DE LAS CASAS is an award-winning author, storyteller, and founder of Picture Book Month, an international literacy initiative that celebrates the print picture book during the month of November. She tours internationally presenting author visit/storytelling programs, educator/librarian training, and workshops. Her performances, dubbed "revved-up storytelling" are full of energetic audience participation. The author of more than twenty books, she writes children's picture books as well as titles with ABC-CLIO/Libraries Unlimited. Visit her website at www.diannedelascasas.com.

STEFAN JOLET grew up in the culturally rich Cajun community of Lafayette, Louisiana. He has had a passion for art since he was a young boy and has been a graphic designer and illustrator for sixteen years. A self-taught artist, he has designed and created promotional materials including posters, flyers, brochures, business cards, and bookmarks. His love of children's books led him to illustrate a picture book titled *The Legend of Peli Claus* by Nolan "Joey" Pellerin. Jolet also illustrated an acclaimed iPad/iPhone app titled "Rockin' Three Billy Goats" by Dianne de Las Casas. Visit his website at www .stefanjolet.com.

Dianne de Las Casas's Libraries Unlimited Titles

Handmade Tales 2: More Stories to Make and Take (Libraries Unlimited, 2013)
Filled with even more draw and tell, fold and tell, cut and tell, string stories, and new extras such as stories with towels, paper bags, paper plates, and more!

A is for Alligators: Draw and Tell Stories from A–Z (Libraries Unlimited, 2011)
Dianne de Las Casas and Marita Gentry team to create a unique ABC book of draw and tell stories that use each letter of the alphabet to create animals kids will love!

Tales from the 7,000 Isles: Filipino Folk Stories (Libraries Unlimited, 2011)
The book, containing Filipino folktales, recipes, crafts, and children's games, is part of Libraries Unlimited's World Folklore Series.

Tell Along Tales: Playing with Participation Tales (Libraries Unlimited, 2011)
"Teachers, public librarians, school librarians, and storytellers will find this book valuable for engaging elementary students. Tips for making storytelling an active learning experience will help even the novice librarian captivate students." —Library Media Connection

Stories on Board: Creating Board Games from Favorite Tales (Libraries Unlimited, 2010)
Students learn to create fun board games with adapted tales from around the world, integrating language arts, math, and social studies.

Scared Silly: 25 Tales to Tickle & Thrill (Libraries Unlimited, 2009)
Winner, Storytelling World Award
A primer on how to tell spooky stories with 25 popular tales. *"A welcome and highly recommended addition to academic library and community library staff resource collections."* —Midwest Book Review

Tangram Tales: Story Theater Using the Ancient Chinese Puzzle (Libraries Unlimited, 2009)
Twenty-five adapted world tales combine language arts and math through the use of tangrams and storytelling. Includes a tangram puzzle!

Handmade Tales: Stories to Make and Take (Libraries Unlimited, 2008) Bestseller!
Filled with string stories, draw and tell, cut and tell, paper tales (fold and tell, roll books, paper fortune-teller tales), and other tales (handkerchiefs, napkins, and towels). Ordinary objects are turned into extraordinary stories!

The Story Biz Handbook: How to Manage Your Storytelling Career from the Desk to the Stage (Libraries Unlimited, 2008)
Winner, Storytelling World Award
The Story Biz Handbook is the ultimate primer on how to become a professional storyteller. *"Wonderful, information-packed resource!"* — Terrence Roberts, professional storyteller (review from Amazon.com)

Kamishibai Story Theater: The Art of Picture Telling (Libraries Unlimited, 2006)
Kamishibai is the Japanese art of storytelling with pictures. An amazing collaborative process, this technique brings out the creativity in each student.

Story Fest: Crafting Story Theater Scripts (Libraries Unlimited, 2005)
Dianne's innovative story theater scripts are designed for whole classroom participation using creative movement, drama, and rhythm instruments.